© 2022 kaleidoscope kids, llc

all rights reserved.

no part of this publication may be reproduced, distributed, or transmitted in any form or by any means, including photocopying or other electronic or mechanical method, without prior written permission of kaleidoscope kids, llc except in the case of brief quotations embodied in critical reviews and certain other noncommercial uses permitted by copyright law. for permission requests, please write to us at hello@readkaleidoscope.com

published in the united states by kaleidoscope kids, llc

visit us at www.readkaleidoscope.com

kaleidoscope, *kids bibles reimagined*

library of congress cataloging-in-publication data is available upon request
ISBN: 979-8-9851532-3-1

cover art by marlena sigman
logo design by morgan carter @bymorgancarter
editing by chris ammen and laurie sibley

For Ellie, Georgia, and all the friends of the Westminster Library. May you hear the echo of the Good King's voice in every true and lovely tale you read.

WELCOME TO KALEIDOSCOPE

First of all, thank you for picking up a copy of Kaleidoscope! We are glad to have you. In the following pages, you'll experience the Bible in a whole new way.

Kaleidoscope was borne from the need to provide a fun, engaging, age-appropriate retelling of the Bible for elementary-aged children to transition them from "little kid" Bibles to adult translations.

At Kaleidoscope, we are producing single volumes for every book of the Bible. They're designed to read like chapter books, so you'll turn pages and look forward with anticipation to the next volume.

But don't let the fact that we are focused on kids deter you if you are a "big kid!" Good children's books are almost always as good for adults as they are for kids.

Get excited! In the pages that follow, you'll see God's wonderful good news. Our prayer is that His kindness, gentleness, and love will melt our hearts and make us more like Jesus.

The Kaleidoscope Team

Holly Mackle's retelling of Esther begins with the looming intrigue of an epic movie trailer and unfurls into one thrilling chapter after another. Truly, every description and teaching moment captivates. Undoubtedly, *Bright Star* will grab your kid's attention with a delightful determination that says, "Look at what God can do!" (Seriously: I nearly applauded at the end.)
-Caroline Saunders, author of *Good News: How to Know the Gospel and Live It* and *Better Than Life: How to Study the Bible and Like It* from LifeWay Girls

I've read Esther dozens of times. But never like this. After each chapter, I found myself wanting to know, "What happens next?" In *Bright Star*, Holly Mackle has created something beautiful, playful, and compelling. And like the hero of this story, the writing absolutely shines.
–Chris Pappalardo, Writer and Co-founder of Advent Blocks

Don't start this one at bedtime unless you're prepared to stay up late! This page turner will have your child begging for "just one more chapter" with wide-eyed wonder. I'm so grateful for an age-appropriate resource to tell a story that's so easy to get wrong (be like Esther—a brave hero!) in a way that winsomely points them instead to the hero they have in King Jesus– the only one who saves.
-Abbey Wedgeworth, author of *Held*, a few children's books (2023), and mom to three boys

Holly Mackle skillfully retells this powerful story of God's saving grace in a way that children will understand and love! With a Christ-centered focus on every page, young readers will learn to see Jesus in the Old Testament through this creative retelling of Esther.
–Amy Gannett, author of *Fix Your Eyes: How our Study of God Shapes Our Worship of Him* and founder of Tiny Theologians

I was on the edge of my seat during this adventurous telling of God's plan to protect His people through Esther. The characters came to life. Big ideas, history, the culture and the God who never changes are explained well for a young reader.
-Katie Flores, PCA Children's Ministry Coordinator

Through vivid storytelling and clear teaching, Holly Mackle draws young readers deep into the story of Esther. There's adventure! Danger! (But not romance, ick!) And an unforgettable ending that points to an even greater Story—one that welcomes all of us to be part of it, forever. Kids and their parents will love *Bright Star: The Story of Esther*!
-Amanda Cleary Eastep, author of the Tree Street Kids middle grade series

CREATORS

Holly Mackle is a lower school librarian, author of the family Advent devotional *Little Hearts, Prepare Him Room*, and curator of the mom humor collaboration *Same Here, Sisterfriend, Mostly True Tales of Misadventures in Motherhood*. Holly and her husband, David, wrangle two young girls in Birmingham, Alabama. Connect with Holly on Instagram @hollymacklebooks.

Marlena Sigman is an artist and designer based in Greenville, South Carolina. She earned a fine arts degree in design at Auburn University, and has a deep love for color, shape, and typography. She finds inspiration in thrift stores, historic buildings, newgrass, and classic literature. If she's not creating art, she's traveling or playing with her dog.

TABLE OF CONTENTS

BRIGHT STAR   1
    ESTHER 1:1-12

ESTHER SHINES   9
    ESTHER 1:13-2:18

ENTER THE VILLAINS   15
    ESTHER 2:19-3:15

TROUBLE   21
    ESTHER 4:1-17

ESTHER SPEAKS FOR HER PEOPLE   25
    ESTHER 5:1-8

A PLAN BACKFIRES   29
    ESTHER 5:9-6:14

THE TRUTH COMES OUT   37
    ESTHER 7:1-8:2

A KIND PROTECTION   41
    ESTHER 8:3-17

THE KING'S FAVOR, GUARANTEED   45
    ESTHER 9:1-10:3

INTRODUCTION

God's people have known their fair share of enemies.

Sixteen hundred years before the story of Esther began, God made an amazing promise to Abraham that He would make a great nation come from his tiny family—a people more numerous than the stars in the sky.

But many enemies would try to ruin that plan.

Five hundred years before Esther lived, the mighty Goliath and the Philistines threatened David and God's people.

Exactly 100 years before Esther, Nebuchadnezzar and the Babylonian empire destroyed God's temple in Jerusalem. They carried God's people far from home and into exile.

And just 60 years earlier, a den of lions all but assured the death of the prophet Daniel.

Now, 60 years after conquering the fearsome Babylonians, there was a new threat to God's people—Persia.

The Persian army was strong, their numbers great, their cities grand, and their dominance unmatched.

In those days, the Persian kings' egos spread as far and wide as their rule and reign. They would stop at nothing to ensure that their own power might increase, guaranteeing the throne for their sons and their sons' sons after them.

But egos and power didn't just stop with the kings. Everyday Persian people were used to getting what they wanted, too. Spoiled and entitled, they had an unquenchable thirst for wealth, power, and beauty.

In those days, there was no room for a "capital-G God" in Persia. And unless He wanted to serve their selfish purposes, there was certainly no space for One who might want to rule over hearts.

Over a century earlier, Nebuchadnezzar and the Babylonian empire captured and scattered God's people far from their homes, where they were slaves in exile for 70 years. When the Persians conquered the Babylonians after those 70 years, a first wave of exiles was allowed to return home to rebuild Jerusalem, their capital city.

After that first return, another 60 years passed. For many reasons, most of God's people remained far from home, in the land of their exile.

They had not returned to worship the One True God in the place and way He'd commanded.

But through 70 years of exile and more—whether they'd returned to Jerusalem or stayed back in Persia—God never left His people. Though many Israelites made their home in a foreign land, God had made His home in their hearts.

In this time, one extraordinary girl, clothed not outwardly but inwardly—in strength and dignity, rose to lead God's people.

This is where the story of Esther begins.

BRIGHT STAR

Esther 1:1-12

Every evening since God created day and night, the same magical events occur. Sometimes we can see them and sometimes not—often it depends on whether or not we're paying attention. Every evening, as the sun burns its last ray of light in our view and sinks just below the horizon, a new sky opens up.

In the stillness, our eyes adjust to the fading colors. First, we notice one faint pop of light and then another. Then, finally, if we have eyes to see, the entire expanse lights up, filled with dazzling, winking stars. As our eyes adjust to behold them, they seem to stand taller, and shine brighter and brighter.

There once lived a girl just like this—a girl who, though she had flowing hair and dazzling eyes, shone more vividly from within. In fact, this girl's name even meant "star." Her circumstances made her a very unexpected heroine, but she was a heroine nonetheless, and her name was Esther.

"Oh, goody!" You might say, "An adventure story!"

And indeed, you would be correct. So cozy up and lean in close, for this is a Bible story unlike any other, with a heroine unlike any other.

But let's not get ahead of ourselves, for this is the story of a hero's journey, and for our hero to emerge, we must first find her in grave danger....

There was once a gigantic empire called Persia that stretched over 127 provinces from India all the way to Ethiopia. Persia's capital, Susa, was full of grand buildings, stylish people, and delicious food.

Susa even had the most powerful leader on earth, King Ahasuerus (pronounced uh-haz-yoo-eer-uhs, and sometimes called King Xerxes). Of course, this majestic leader threw the best parties in all the land. One of his wild shindigs even lasted for six months!

At the end of one of these especially long parties, the king invited his closest friends to stay for some extra fun. Curtains flowing like waterfalls surrounded the splendid room, and candlelight danced off the golden goblets. Tables dripped with delicacies brought in from all over the empire, and pitchers overflowed with the finest wines. King Ahasuerus really must have had it all... or did he?

You may not find it terribly surprising that this was a false empire, a hollow shell of a kingdom where all the power, beauty, and wealth hid a far darker truth.

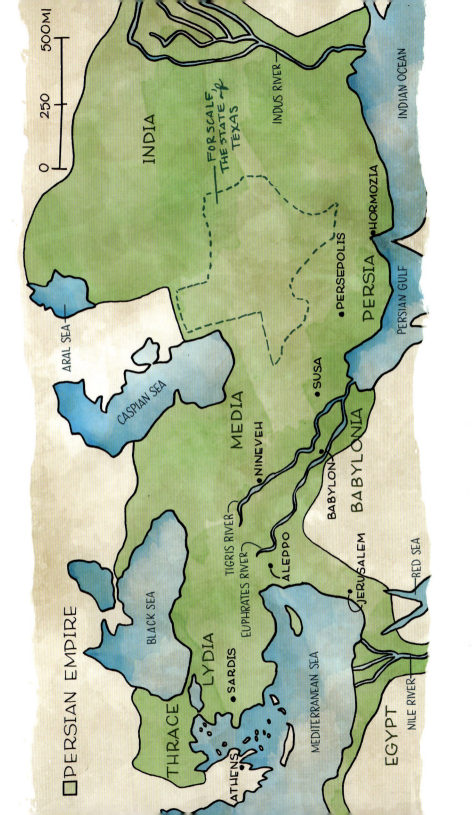

Behind Persia's greatness was a terrible place, full of empty people who lived only for themselves—foolish, faithless, heartless, and ruthless.

After seven days of eating and drinking, the king sent word to his wife, Queen Vashti. He asked her to appear before the king and his friends so that they might appreciate her beauty.

But Queen Vashti said, "No."

The wind calmed as the sun dipped beneath the horizon. The night stilled into a silence so quiet that Vashti's "no" echoed throughout the empire. No one denied the king, not even the queen.

Maybe Queen Vashti was frustrated with the king's behavior and his friends' willingness to go along with it. Perhaps she didn't want to leave the party she was throwing nearby. Or it's possible she didn't feel like being paraded around; maybe she wanted to send a message to the king that he couldn't treat her this way. But for reasons we don't know and may never fully understand until heaven—Queen Vashti said, "No."

Queen Vashti's refusal made the king embarrassed and very upset. As his cheeks stung, his throat closed up, and his chest tightened, the king realized he was far more than angry or upset. He was actually enraged.

So enraged that anger burned his skin like the blazing Persian sun.

"How dare the queen refuse me?" he scoffed.

"The queen disrespects us all, my lord," retorted one of his men, just as confounded as the king. "Once all the other ladies in the kingdom hear about this, they'll think, 'If Queen Vashti can do it, so can I!' They'll all start saying 'no' to the men in their lives, too, and we can NOT have that!"

A roar boiled over among the king's men.

"Something must be done!" cried one.

"Women must know their place!" shouted another.

"My lord, if I may," one of the men chimed in. "A letter should be written and sent to all the empire that Queen Vashti is never to appear before the king again. She must be banished, and a new queen found—a better queen—one who respects the master of her household and honors the king!"

King Ahasuerus stroked his beard and considered his options. What to do with the disagreeable Queen Vashti? It didn't take long for the king to agree with his friends, and together they hatched a plan. The queen would be stripped of her status and never allowed to come into the king's presence again.

Furthermore, the king proclaimed to his 127 provinces that all women should obey their husbands, no matter what!

Kaleidoscope Corner
Godly Submission

Do you ever find the Bible confusing?

Often when we read the Bible, it's difficult to remember or even understand that each book of the Bible takes place during a time in history that's very different from our own. Culture changes constantly—but God doesn't. So when we read the Bible, we can try to understand cultural factors and seek to know God, whose heart is always the same toward us.

In much of Bible times, women were considered second-class citizens, under male authority in every way. If a woman had a kind or God-fearing male authority (husband, father, or cousin, as we will see with Esther), she likely enjoyed many freedoms. But if her male authority was not kind or God-fearing, she probably lived under difficult or even threatening circumstances.

Jesus turned the world upside down in just about every way, including how people should honor one another. He made friends with women, hugged children, and dined at the homes of outcasts.

The apostle Paul, under the inspiration of the Holy Spirit, turned the concept of godly submission upside-down. In Ephesians 5, Paul remarks that we are all called to honor one another in love, as we all obey God. No one should blindly follow another person. Husbands should not force their wives to do anything disrespectful. Instead, they should treat their wives with dignity and honor, even better than the husband treats himself, as this is how Jesus loves us.

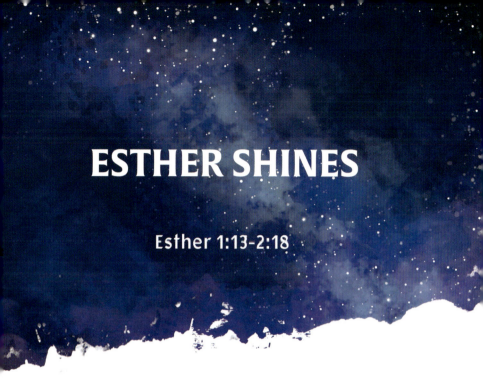

ESTHER SHINES

Esther 1:13-2:18

It took a while for the king's anger to subside, but when it did, he found a root of bitterness toward Queen Vashti firmly planted in his heart. Wanting to calm the king's rage, his friends suggested he appoint officers in each province to gather the most beautiful young women to find a replacement for Vashti. The women would be brought to Susa and placed in the care of Hegai, the king's assistant.

Hegai would see that they received beauty treatments, fine clothing, and all the makeup they could imagine—for an entire year! It would take all that time to prepare them, for only the most radiant woman would suit the king.

The proclamation went out, and the search began for a queen who would honor the great king.

In the capital city of Susa, where the king lived, there also lived a Jew named Mordecai, who was a follower of the God of Israel (Israel is another name for God's people). In the days of Abraham, Isaac, and Jacob, Jews lived in their homeland, Israel. However, many years before Mordecai was born, King Nebuchadnezzar of Babylon conquered Israel. He kicked out the Jewish people (remember Daniel and his friends?). Nebuchadnezzar sent the Israelites into exile, where they lived far from home in many other lands.

That's how Mordecai and his younger cousin, named Hadassah, both Jews, wound up living in Persia rather than Israel. Mordecai was a kind and caring man and adopted Hadassah as his daughter.

Hadassah was beautiful, with fine eyes and a graceful form. Mordecai and Hadassah's hearts broke at King Ahasuerus's proclamation. They knew Hadassah would be called to the palace to become a part of the king's selection.

Should her true identity be revealed, Hadassah would be in certain danger inside the walls of the palace since the empire allowed no room for a God who claimed to be the One True God—the God of Abraham, Isaac, and Jacob.

The name Hadassah was a dead giveaway that Esther was an Israelite. For her protection, Hadassah and Mordecai changed her name to Esther, which means "hidden" in Hebrew and "star" in Persian.

Once inside the palace, the competition began. Each young woman had one opportunity with the king—just one chance to win his favor and become Persia's new queen. With 127 provinces, there were at least 127 beautiful young women competing for the king's attention!

As Hegai (who was assigned to look after all the women and oversee their treatments) surveyed the new arrivals, one stood out in particular: Esther—one dimly shining glimmer of light. Hegai decided to look after Esther and provide her with all she needed, plus additional fine food, makeup, the best room in the house, and young women to serve her. All the while, Esther kept her true identity a secret.

Day after day, Mordecai paced in front of the palace court where the young women spent their days, listening and asking any insiders who passed by—begging for news about Esther.

As the months of preparation passed, Esther waited and waited, watching beautiful, bejeweled women come and go before her day arrived. Since it was custom for each woman to select treasures and fine clothing, spices and jewelry from the king's collection, Hegai, out of kindness and delight in her, instructed Esther on what to wear and how to fix her hair. He guided Esther toward what he knew would please the king. Esther listened to his advice.

The evening arrived—it was Esther's turn! The shimmering star brightened, then stepped into the presence and full view of royalty.

Of course, it's no surprise that Esther, having already won the favor of everyone she met since stepping foot inside the palace, also won the favor of King Ahasuerus.

He knew she was the one and set a sparkling crown on her head. Then, the king proclaimed Esther the new Queen of Persia and threw a huge party—Esther's Feast, he called it.

He even declared the day a holiday throughout his kingdom and gave gifts to people everywhere. Esther shone and shone, the king's choice of bride, the beauty of Persia delighted in by all, the star of the empire.

"But I thought you said this was an adventure story!?" you might say.

"Where's the adventure? Where's the danger? So far, it's nothing but an icky love story."

Ah, but you would be correct— no story has real stakes without the plotting of an evil villain.

ENTER THE VILLAINS

Esther 2:19-3:15

Not long after Esther was named queen, her cousin Mordecai was standing at the palace gate when he overheard two of the guards plotting to kill the king! As this was a life or death situation for the king (and possibly a credit to him for reporting the plot), Mordecai told Esther immediately. Esther then delivered the news to the king, giving Mordecai credit for discovering it.

The Persian officials investigated and found that the men were indeed plotting to murder the king, and they punished them with death. Mordecai's faithfulness to the king was written in an official document called the Book of the Chronicles—a history book of the empire.

> These two would-be murderers weren't ever the real threat, however. No, they were just the warm-up act, quickly to be forgotten. But it's Mordecai's faithfulness in protecting the king that you should file away in your memory for later on.

In those days, there lived an especially wicked man named Haman. He's the real villain of our story!

Haman was a descendant of Agag, an evil king from another Bible story found in 1 Samuel 15. Ever since the days of Samuel, the Agagites and the Israelites hated each other.

The wicked Haman was an official in the king's palace, but what's worse is that King Ahasuerus thought Haman was one of the good guys and just kept promoting him. Haman was promoted so high that eventually the king told all the people they had to bow down to him and honor him in addition to the king.

But Mordecai knew who Haman was—he'd learned of his hatred for God's people. And so, day after day, Mordecai refused to bow down to Haman, saying, "I am a Jew and do not bow to anyone other than the One True God."

Finally, the royal officials told Haman about Mordecai's refusal, saying to each other, "Let's see what Haman is going to do about this Jew not bowing down to him. This should be fun."

Now it was Haman's turn to burn with rage. He became so angered that his fury didn't stop with Mordecai—Haman promised to kill not just Mordecai but all the Jews in Persia!

Haman went to King Ahasuerus to put his plan into motion. "Oh mighty king," Haman began, "there are people in your land who do not obey your laws. They believe there is a kingdom higher than yours, a god greater than you. But, oh great one, we all know this cannot possibly be true."

"Oh really?" Haman had the king's attention.

"Decree that they be destroyed, and I will pay you lots and lots of money."

In the king's mind, Haman's math was quite favorable:

> Gobs of money + boasting of his awesomeness + getting rid of a group of people who didn't think he was the most awesome = a great plan!

The king took off his royal ring and gave it to Haman the Agagite, the enemy of the Jews, and issued the dark blessing, "Do what seems good to you."

Haman knew just what seemed good to him—he plotted that all Jews, men and women, young and old, should be killed in eleven months—all in one day, in all 127 provinces. Haman got to work quickly. He knew just what to do with the king's ring—just how to seal the fate of Israel with his stamp of death.

The messengers' horses snarled and stomped as they rode toward all the far-reaching provinces with Haman's wicked plan on their hearts and in their mouths. As the Jews learned of the fateful plan, they turned their eyes to the heavens, to the blinking stars, wondering if all was lost. Had God forgotten them? Had He finally left them, sure to be swallowed whole by the plans of the wicked?

Kaleidoscope Corner
Enmity

Can you think of people in the Bible who are enemies?

From the fall in Genesis 3 and onward, Scripture is filled with one group of people hating another—most often a group disliking the people of God, Israel. This aggressive, open hatred of another person or group is called "enmity."

Much of the book of Esther is the result of the enmity between the Agagites and the Jews. Many years before Esther, God told King Saul to destroy the Amalekites because of their hatred for God's people. Saul obeyed God's instructions... to a point. But he disobeyed in leaving Agag, king of the Amalekites, alive. As a result, Agag's offspring would continue to hate the Jews and seek their destruction, becoming long-time enemies. Haman was a descendant of Agag.

Enmity is not unique to Bible characters. Without the grace and redemption of Jesus, each of us would be filled with it, hating and destroying one another. The book of James teaches us that we're to have enmity toward one thing only—sin and wickedness. (James 4:4)

The Persians practiced divination, or deciding days for important events based on something seemingly random, like throwing dice. But, instead of dice, they tossed "pur," or small fragments of stone or pottery. Haman cast these stones (see the illustration on the next page) to decide the date for his murderous plot to be carried out—when he would completely wipe out the Jews from Persia. The stones fell on the twelfth month, nearly one year from then. So, Haman believed he had one year to plot the downfall of God's people.

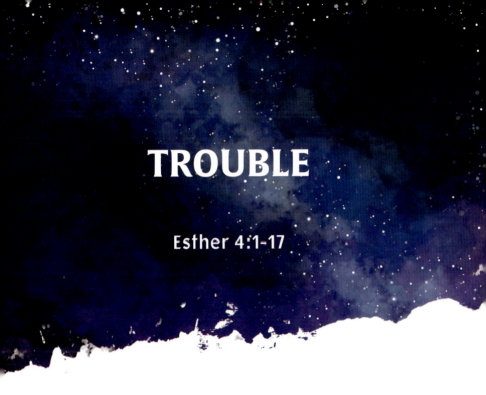

TROUBLE

Esther 4:1-17

Mordecai stilled as he heard the news, an icy rush coursing through his veins. In deep sorrow, he tore his clothing, dressed in rags, poured ash on his head, and walked to the center of Susa, where he uttered a deep and mournful cry.

Knowing he couldn't see Esther, still he walked up to the king's gate—unable to pass through as it was against the law to go in dressed as he was—but he had to get Esther a message.

Esther's attendants ran to him, recognizing Mordecai and seeing his panicked expression. "Please," uttered Mordecai through the bars at the gate, "you have to tell her."

Esther was in shock at the news. Worried for Mordecai, she sent her servants back with clothing to cover him, but he refused. Mordecai doubled down—Esther was missing the urgency! Barely able to get the words out, Mordecai told the queen's messengers all the details of Haman's wicked plot—the money, the decree, the destruction of the Jews.

He sent a copy of the decree back to Esther with her messengers. With the evidence at hand, Mordecai urged Esther to risk her life by going to the king without being called. She must beg for mercy for Israel!

"Now, wait a second!" you might say. "Aren't the king and Esther married? So, why can't she see him whenever she wants?" (And you would be correct in thinking this is a very silly thing indeed.) But at that time in history, and especially in the Persian empire, a king could get rid of his wife for any reason he wanted. King Ahasuerus had done just that when Queen Vashti said, "No," to him. So, that explains why if Esther were to go to see the king uninvited, she would be in great....

DANGER!

You see, in Persia there was one law that you simply didn't break: if you went into the king's inner courts without being called, you were sure to be put to death. Your only hope was the unlikely event that the king would miraculously show mercy, hold out his golden scepter, and spare your life.

Esther shook with fear—the king hadn't called her to his inner courts for 30 days. There was no guarantee that she'd be safe, even as the queen. Esther trembled as she shared her fears with Mordecai.

Mordecai replied with the harsh truth, "Do not think that your fate will be different just because you live in the king's palace. You will not escape because of your position. And if you do not speak for us, God will save us another way, but you will die. Isn't it possible, my dear Hadassah, that you rose to your position as the queen for such a time as this? You are Esther now, and God can use you to guide your people to safety."

Esther steadied herself, wiped her tears, straightened her royal robes, and prepared for the fearsome task. Esther instructed Mordecai to ask all the Jews in Susa to pray for her day and night. They would go without food for three days so their hungry bellies would remind them to beg God for the salvation of His people.

Likewise, Esther and her attendants would also fast, or go without food for a set amount of time. Together, they would cry out to God from inside and outside the palace walls. Esther resolved that after the three days of fasting had passed, she would walk beyond the grand gates into the king's inner courts. Uniquely placed for such a time as this, Esther would plead her case. She would risk her life for her people.

"We shall fast and pray together," Esther resolved, "and after the fast, I will go to the king, though it is against the law of the empire. If it's the end of my days, then so be it. If I perish, I perish."

In the dark skies above Susa, now one solitary star stood seemingly alone, brighter than all the others. Shaky at first, then steadier, as if urged on by a force far behind and beyond it, powered by something that came not from outward appearances, but from within.

ESTHER SPEAKS FOR HER PEOPLE

Esther 5:1-8

As Esther's attendants dressed her for the all-important hour, she caught sight of her reflection, took a deep breath, and steadied her heart to the task. No longer Hadassah, the little Jewish orphan, Esther stood taller and braver than before. She knew what she had to do. Esther called for her royal robes, a reminder to the king of the very day he'd set the crown on her head, lifting Esther above all others.

Once again, a hush fell. But this time, just over the throne room as Esther walked toward the king. Clothed in strength and dignity, she stepped toward her husband and her king, knowing her life could end in just one moment. But Esther stood tall. She approached the king's inner court without worry or apology, for a star is not ashamed that it shines.

When the king looked up, the radiant Esther startled him. She was certainly out of place, inviting herself into the king's inner court. This was against the law—what would he do?

Would he remember the star he once chose above all the others? Would he spare her life or keep the scepter at his side and give her the penalty of death.

Esther slowly raised her eyes from the floor where they'd been out of respect for the king. She saw his arm extend and felt his eyes lock on hers, piercing and unclear. And then King Ahasuerus raised his golden scepter. Relief washed over Esther. She was saved!

"My dear queen," said the king, "What troubles you? Tell me what you need. I promise—up to half my kingdom is yours."

Confidence rose from Esther's heart to her head at her husband's overwhelming generosity. She breathed deep, "My king, I'd like to prepare a feast for you. Please come, and please bring Haman."

"Quickly!" shouted the king toward his servants. "Gather Haman, for the lovely Queen Esther will have her request!"

Haman was more than delighted to join the king as Esther's guest of honor. That evening, the two men ate and drank their fill, feasting on all manner of delicious food.

"Queen Esther," the king addressed her directly. "While this is surely a fine feast, I can hardly imagine you invited us simply to honor us with this food and your radiant presence." The king studied Esther's face. "No, there's something more. Tell me, my dear. There's something that troubles you. I must ask you again, what is your request? Surely you cannot doubt that up to half my kingdom shall be yours if only you ask."

"My king," replied Esther, "my plea is that you and Haman return tomorrow for yet another feast, and tomorrow I will tell you my request."

"Now, wait a second," you might interrupt, and that would be well within your rights as a curious noticer-of-details.

"Didn't Esther invite the king to the feast so she could tell him how bad Haman was? Why is she waiting?"

Excellent questions, indeed. I'd love to tell you. Listen close, for it's one of the Bible's biggest secrets....

We don't know.

I wish we did. Oodles of Bible scholars have tried to determine why Esther did what she did. But for reasons we don't know and may never fully understand until heaven, Esther asked the men to come back the next day. And the king and Haman, being enthusiastic fans of wine and feasting and parties, were very happy to do so.

A PLAN BACKFIRES

Esther 5:9-6:14

Haman didn't walk out of Esther's feast; he glided out. Chest puffed, cheeks red from too much wine, eyes glistening from far too much merriment, Haman made haste toward his house. He couldn't wait to tell his wife, Zeresh, and all his friends how he'd been invited not once —but twice—to be the honored guest of the lovely queen!

On his way, what stomped on his good mood but that horrid Mordecai! The Jew who would not rise and bow before him! Did Mordecai not know that Haman was coming from the queen's presence? Did he not see the cloud of royalty hanging around him?

Oh, that Mordecai! The very bane of Haman's existence. Haman stared in Mordecai's direction, and wouldn't you know, Mordecai neither stood nor trembled before him.

Haman's wrath bubbled. But first, there was bragging to do. He decided to deal with him later.

Once home, Haman left no stone unturned in entertaining his listeners with the fine details of the feast. But Haman didn't stop there—after the tale of the meal, Haman continued, being sure his listeners were reminded of his riches, his handsome sons, and all the ways the king had honored him. No memory was left unremembered, and no guest unreminded of Haman's extraordinariness.

"And did you know I'm invited again tomorrow?" Haman reminded his friends for the 30th time.

"All by myself, just me and the king." Despite it all, something burned on Haman's tongue—it was that dreaded Mordecai, daring not to stand and honor him and stealing his joy on the very day he was the honored palace guest!

"Something must be done with Mordecai," Haman told his friends.

"Easy peasy!" said his wife, Zeresh. "Here's what you do: set a hanging place to kill Mordecai. Then, hang him!"

Zeresh's laugh cracked and stabbed. "Do it tomorrow morning! Then you can enjoy your feast knowing he's long gone."

Haman was delighted with the plan and had the gallows (another name for the hanging place) built that very night—as tall as four giraffes stacked on top of each other! That way, everyone could see what happens to somcone who refuses to give honor where it's due, the same thing that would happen to all Jews in Persia in a few short months.

The king tossed and turned on his bed all night, unable to sleep. Finally he gave up, rose, and called for his servants to bring him the Book of the Chronicles—something snoozy to lull him back to dreamland. As the king listened to a servant read the book aloud, a familiar name caught his attention...

...Mordecai!

"Wait, go back. Did you say, Mordecai?!"

"Yes, my lord. Here it's written that Mordecai reported that two of the king's guards wanted to lay hands on you and kill you."

"And what honor did Mordecai receive for this act of service and bravery?"

The servants looked back and forth from one to another, eyebrows up, hoping someone could remember something, anything, that they could tell the king.

Then, finally, after what seemed like an eternity, one spoke: "I suppose nothing, my lord."

"Who of my men is in the court at this very moment—I must make this right for the faithful Mordecai."

Now of all the people—all the people!—who you'd guess would enter the king's court right at that moment, could you ever have imagined in your wildest dreams that the person available to make the king's wish to honor Mordecai come true would be....

"Ah, my dear Haman," the king began, seeing Haman come toward him. "What should be done for a man who has proven himself faithful, loyal, and true—a selfless servant of the king?"

Yes! It's true—it just so happened that the wicked Haman had just entered the court, on his way to ask the king if he could kill Mordecai.

And so it happened that for very different purposes, the king and Haman met face to face, in the middle of a sleepless night, to discuss the fate of Mordecai.

Loyal and true! Faithful! Selfless servant! Thought Haman as a deep breath puffed his chest proud. *Ho ho—The king could only be speaking of me!*

Haman's mind spun quickly—what were the very best of the best honors to suggest?

"For this great man, oh good king, honor him with the finest royal robes—the very ones you have worn before! And let these robes be draped over him just before he is put on one of the king's horses with a crown—a crown!—on the horse's head!

"And...and...hand the reigns of the horse to one of the noblest of the king's officials so that he may lead this great man through the busiest part of the city calling out, 'The king desires to honor this man!' so that all may hear of his greatness."

"You've got it, Haman, my good man! What a wonderful idea! Go immediately, take the items you have said and place them on Mordecai the Jew. You are just the person to lead Mordecai and the royal steed throughout Susa's streets. Use your loudest, most booming voice so that all may hear of the honor of Mordecai and how he protected my life! Now, Haman, go quickly!"

Haman froze, humiliation rising into a lump in his throat and reddening his cheeks. This conversation had not gone the way he'd expected.

And so it came to pass that the wicked Haman planned the most desirable honor for his enemy, Mordecai, just as he would have selected for himself!

When it was all over, Haman returned home, covered in embarrassment and anger. Through hot tears, Haman told his wife and all his family about the day's events. Then, Haman's closest friends saw the writing on the wall. "Oh, Haman, this will not end well for you."

Just then, some messengers from the king arrived to bring Haman to the feast—the second feast that Esther had prepared for Haman and the king.

THE TRUTH COMES OUT

Esther 7:1-8:2

Queen Esther's heart was tense, marking every move—every word between the king and Haman. She was hyper-aware of the timing of her request as they reclined at the table, bellies full of the feast and hearts joyful with wine.

Again, the king questioned Esther, "My queen, do tell me what your wish is. You've entertained us with the finest food and your brilliant company. You may ask anything of me. Once more, I promise that whatever you ask—up to half my kingdom is yours."

Esther breathed in. The weight of her people's request was heavy on her heart. This was the moment. The night stilled in anticipation. The star rose to speak.

"My king, I want to ask for the protection of myself and my people."

"Protection? Why ever would you need protection? Esther, you are safe within these walls."

"No, my king." Esther clasped her hands and shook her head. "There is a plot against us. If it were simply a plot to enslave us, I would not trouble you with the details. But the plot is not to enslave us, but to murder us! My people were sold—and the purchaser wants to end our lives!"

"Who is he, and where is he? Bring him to me now!" the kind demanded.

While the stars shone bright and vibrant above the gates of Susa, it was the star inside the palace walls that shone even brighter.

The king's fury fueled Esther's confidence. She must finish the task. "This hatred is within one of your own men! It is Haman, my lord!"

Haman froze in fear. The king stood up, pounded his fists on the table, and stormed off, heading in the direction of the palace garden. The king's silence was worse than his screaming.

The hairs on the back of Haman's neck stood on end. He moved quickly to spare his own neck. Haman fell at Esther's feet, pleading for his life, begging, bargaining, promising—anything to get Esther to change the king's mind, for Haman knew the king would be bent on ending his life.

In one last, final act of desperation, Haman fell onto the couch where Queen Esther was seated just as the king returned from the garden.

"In my own house?!" shouted the king as the guards removed Haman from the palace.

"My lord," one of the king's guards spoke up. "Haman prepared gallows for Mordecai outside his house. He was going to ask your permission to hang Mordecai."

"Well, how convenient," retorted the king. "This devil shall hang from his own gallows."

And so, just like that, death turned back on itself. Haman met his end in just the way he had intended to destroy God's people, Israel. And everyone was there to see it.

On that very day, King Ahasuerus gave all the property and riches of Haman to Queen Esther.

She, in turn, gave them to Mordecai. Additionally, the king removed a kingly ring from his finger and gave it to Mordecai—a sign of trust and honor.

And quick as a wink, you would think that our story would end, right? Danger avoided, the beautiful queen saved, the faithful man honored, good winning over evil—haven't we checked all the boxes?

Perhaps our limited, human boxes.

But not when it comes to God and His promises. And God clearly wasn't finished.

A KIND PROTECTION

Esther 8:3-17

With Haman now gone, all should have been well, but it wasn't. Haman had set in motion a plan of action for the whole kingdom. From India to Ethiopia, all the Jews were to be put to death on the 13th day of the 12th month. Esther's job was not yet complete.

She fell at the feet of the king, wetting his feet with her tears. She was safe, but now she must plead for the safety of her people.

But there was a big problem—a really big problem. A king's ruling could not be overturned! Not even by another law from the king! Something must be done. There had to be a way out. But what?

At the king's invitation, Esther and Mordecai devised a plan—a simultaneous order from the king to go alongside the first. While it couldn't stop the enemies of Israel from attacking the Jews, this time the Jews would be allowed to fight back. But more than the ability to defend themselves, the plan gave them plenty of time to gather supplies, train soldiers, and make a strategy.

Mordecai constructed this order under the protective eye of the king and sealed it with that famous seal, the king's ring. This time, the king's own horses rode swiftly in the direction of all 127 provinces. They carried word of the ruling, each one written in the language of its recipients, far and wide, spreading the news that all Jews could gather and defend themselves.

The Jews wept with joy and hugged one another at the news. They had been living in utter fear of each passing day since they first learned of Haman's edict. This was the word of rescue they'd been hoping for—God's continued protection of His people.

When Mordecai appeared outside the palace in Susa, a great cheer arose from the crowd. The Jews surrounded him, basking in the glow of hope they hadn't felt in hundreds of years. Finally, someone had spoken up for them. And more importantly, God—their good and eternal King—had remembered them.

Mordecai appeared in fine royal robes of deep blue and white, a crown from the king set atop his head, and a cape of purple linen falling down his back. Mordecai—a Jew—had been dressed as a king, by the very king himself, the one who once signed a law that could have killed Mordecai and all his people.

The Jews prepared a great feast and declared a holiday. Many outsiders saw the might and greatness of the Lord God on behalf of His people and announced that they wanted to follow God as well!

Kaleidoscope Corner
Sovereignty and Providence

God is in charge of everything that happens in all of life. God's "in charge-ness" is what we call His sovereignty.

In the book of Esther, we see so much of God's sovereignty! We also see a part of God known as His providence. This is His special care for His children as a part of all that sovereignty.

God doesn't just plan all the little pieces of the lives of His children—He plans them in such a way so that everything will eventually bring Him the most glory and us the most good. Providence is God's promise that all things will turn out for ultimate good if only we have eyes to see God's "in charge-ness" over all things.

Just like we saw with Joseph in Genesis 50—what people mean for evil, God intends for good—in the book of Esther, it's the very same. Every casting off of a queen, every overlooked mention in a history book, every roll of the pur, every relentless pursuit by God's enemies, every timid step into the presence of a king—everything (everything!) is not just under God's control, but also under the shield of God's kindness toward His people.

And we can rest in that same kind providence today.

THE KING'S FAVOR, GUARANTEED

Esther 9:1-10:3

Get ready for the grand finale...
because just like any great adventure story,
it's time for the big switcheroo!

When the day arrived—the thirteenth day of the twelfth month—the Jews rose to defend themselves. They gathered in cities throughout all the provinces and stomped down the very wickedness that had planned to hunt them.

Haman's story echoed throughout the land as evil was once again hung on its own gallows. King Ahasuerus's guards and officials even helped them by providing weapons and horses, following the instructions of Mordecai, the king's new right-hand man.

In Susa alone, 500 men, including the sons of Haman, were put to death that day at the hands of the Jews. But the Jews knew it wasn't their hands at work. Instead, it was the protective hand of God.

This same hand had carried His people across the Red Sea and out of Egypt, made the way to the Promised Land, and cleared it of enemies. This was the very hand that spread God's people far and wide to cities like Susa so that His power and might could be on display for such a time as this.

Yes, tracing God's protective hand takes many twists and turns, but if you follow the line, there is no doubt of His heart. God is committed to the protection of His people.

The king was stunned when he heard that 500 had died in Susa. He turned to Esther and marveled at the number of people that hated the Jews so much they would seek their destruction.

If King Ahasuerus had any doubt of the danger the Jews were under, surely this number put those doubts to rest.

In yet another act of honor toward Queen Esther, King Ahasuerus asked again, "Esther, what is your wish? Up to half my kingdom, and I will give it to you."

"The work is not done," she replied. "There are many in Susa who still hate my people, and they will not stop the fighting after just one day, I'm sure of it. If it pleases the king, give us another day to protect ourselves."

The following day, the fourteenth day of the twelfth month, 300 more of Susa's men were killed. And throughout all the 127 provinces? A total of 75,000 of Israel's enemies were killed. And the Israelites stole nothing from their enemies (for they remembered the evil that had come upon their forefathers, like Saul).

On the fifteenth day, after two days of intense fighting, all the Jews of Susa held a great feast, with much fine food and dancing and celebrating, for their hearts were joyful.

They were carried through the Red Sea, led through the wilderness, brought into the Promised Land, and now had been saved once again from their enemies.

Why? Because God had a big plan.

Mordecai sat down again to write to the people of all the provinces. This time, though, it was for a very different reason.

"A holiday!" he decreed. "A holiday we shall have! A day of feasting and joyfulness and the giving of gifts to one another and the poor. And we shall remember God's rescue and celebrate His protection over us."

He called this holiday Purim, meaning lots, for the wicked Haman had cast pur (stones) to determine the day of their destruction by mere chance. But God, the perfect King, made a powerful plan to direct even the smallest stone. All the Jews throughout the land determined that they would hold these two days as a celebration to remember what God had done for them.

Queen Esther sealed this celebratory plan with her own authority. The horses rode out to all 127 provinces one final time, this time with words of peace, joy, and gladness. They scattered the light of God's goodness as displayed in his chosen servant, Esther, the Jewish orphan and adopted daughter of Mordecai, and set in place the annual celebration of Purim, a time for celebrating the un-doing of death.

Once again, the faithfulness of Mordecai the Jew was recorded in the Book of the Chronicles. However, this time, the story of the orphan girl Hadassah, turned brilliant star Esther, was found right alongside his.

Their story of courage, bravery, and heart is still celebrated today in the Jewish community and is still called Purim.

But the best part of the entire story of Esther arrives at the very end. In the final line, it's as if God knowingly winks at His readers to show us a hint of what's to come.

Though brilliant, both Esther and Mordecai were mere shadows of what was to come—a star not yet visible in the night sky—a star infinitely better and brighter than all the others:

Jesus, the Bright Morning Star.

Hundreds of years after Esther walked the earth, the birth of the One True Star, Jesus, would be spotted and followed by some very wise men—stargazers—likely from the same region of Persia as Esther.

They would bring the baby Jesus gifts—gold, frankincense, and myrrh—for He was the King who would save His people from their sins. And they would know He was the One who would truly seek, as the final line of the book of Esther states, the welfare and peace of all His people.

Kaleidoscope Corner
Esther Points to Jesus

Esther is much like the star the wise men followed to find the baby Jesus—she pointed the way to the One True Star.

Bright as she was, Esther only foreshadowed Jesus. Like Esther, Jesus, also known as the Bright Morning Star, speaks to God, our King, begging for our protection. And His death on the cross guaranteed that we will always have it.

News of this star, Jesus, would likewise spread far and wide—far wider than the 127 provinces of Persia. The good news, the gospel, spread first to the church in Acts and then through history to us, His modern-day church.

He continues to say to us, His children, "Remember! Remember who I am and celebrate what I've done for you. Trace the glimmers of light in your life back to My hand, your Good King, your Star."

The good news of Jesus lights up our hearts with hope, peace, and gladness. The One True Star gives us ultimate protection from our enemies: sin, Satan, and the world's brokenness. He alone offers eternal rest and the end of all fear.

In all her brilliance, Esther was only a shadow. She was a dim reflection of the true star, Jesus, who wants to shine brightly within each of us.

Resources That Shaped Bright Star

Ash, Christopher. "On Teaching Esther." Interview by Nancy Guthrie. Help Me Teach the Bible, November 6, 2019.

Brown, Paige. "Bible History Overview: Old Testament." Bible Study series, West End Community Church, Nashville, Tennessee, winter 2021.

Esther overview videos. BibleProject.com. 2015-2021.

Harrick, Kristie. Personal study of Esther and Malachi as Bible Study preparation. Briarwood Presbyterian Church. 2019, 2021.

Scott, Jack B. *The Post-Exilic Period in Jerusalem: Adult Biblical Education Series, Vol. II, Book 10*. Atlanta: CDM, 1980.

Scott, Jack B. *The Remnant in Exile: Adult Biblical Education Series, Vol. II Book 9*. Atlanta: CDM, 1980.

Swindoll, Charles. *Esther, A Woman of Strength & Dignity*. Nashville: Thomas Nelson, 1997.

Vos, Catherine. *The Child's Story Bible*. Grand Rapids: Wm. B. Eerdmans, 1977.

Acknowledgments

All my gratitude to Cara Johnson—I am better because of her talented editorial skill and forever changed by her extraordinary friendship.

Special thanks to Kristie Harrick for her wisdom, generosity with her own work, and thoughtful read.

Inspirational gratitude goes to Jess Ray and her beautiful song "Gallows," which rang in my ears during the writing of this Esther account. I hope you'll listen and remember our hope.

And because the process is the best part, I am grateful for the insight and encouragement of Lauren Denton, Meg Flowers, Christina Fox, Anna Gresham, Melany Guzzo, Marlys Roos, Elizabeth Santelmann, and Mrs. Moffett's second-grade class.

What fun to write for Kaleidoscope—thank you to the visionary Chris Ammen, the talented Marlena Sigman, and the whole incredible team.

And to my family, David, Ellie, and Georgia—I love living in these pleasant boundary lines alongside you. Thank you for your constant love and enthusiastic support.